A Very
POMPOM
CHRISTMAS

A Very
POMPOM
CHRISTMAS

20 FESTIVE PROJECTS TO MAKE

Jemima Schlee

First published 2017 by
Guild of Master Craftsman Publications Ltd
Castle Place, 166 High Street, Lewes,
East Sussex, BN7 1XU, UK

ISBN 978 1 78494 387 5

A catalogue record for this book is available from
the British Library.

PUBLISHER Jonathan Bailey
PRODUCTION MANAGER Jim Bulley
SENIOR PROJECT EDITOR Wendy McAngus
EDITOR Sarah Doughty
MANAGING ART EDITOR Gilda Pacitti
DESIGN & ART DIRECTION Wayne Blades
PHOTOGRAPHER Neal Grundy

Colour origination by GMC Reprographics
Printed and bound in Turkey

CONTENTS

INTRODUCTION

What is it about pompoms that brings a smile to your face? For me, they summon up memories of childhood, festivals and celebrations. Just like hanging bunting across a room, pompoms add cheer to whatever they adorn, whether it's parcels, gloves, hats or rooms.

Traditionally constructed using just a couple of discs of card, scraps of yarn and a pair of scissors, making your own pompoms gives you the means to personalize gifts and embellish the ordinary at the most festive time of year – Christmas. What's more, it's fun!

There's a certain magic, whatever your age, in the metamorphic transformation of a tight, wound bundle of yarn to a soft, light fluffy ball. And once you have released that shaggy, soft ball, your scissors come into play, sculpting and teasing the shape and character of your very own creation.

Jemima

TREE DECORATIONS

CHRISTMAS PUDDING

An iconic symbol of a traditional Christmas, this cute little pudding bauble is quick and magical to make. The addition of tiny red berry bells and a couple of felt leaves tops it off perfectly.

YOU WILL NEED
Oddments of black, brown, muddy green, beige and white DK yarns
2½in (6.5cm) pompom maker
Green embroidery thread and needle
Small scraps of green felt
Small, sharp scissors
Knitting needle (or similar blunt tool)
3 x ¼in (6mm) red bells

Tip Tie a little name tag to the hanging loop to make a Christmas table placement for your guests. This is a special something they can take home to hang on their own Christmas tree.

1 Wrap and fill one half of your pompom maker with an assortment of yarn. Use five colours together – such as one black, two brown, one muddy green and one beige. This will create the speckled bottom half of your pudding.

2 Wrap and fill the other half of your pompom maker with white yarn to create the topping. Close, cut and tie the pompom with a length of white yarn before releasing it from the pompom maker. Give it a good, hard trim with small, sharp scissors, retaining the white tie yarn tails.

3 Use the end of the knitting needle (and your fingers) to push and manipulate the line where your speckled pudding base meets the white top. This should create a wavy edge where the two contrasting halves join.

4 Cut two small leaves from the green felt scraps using the templates below. Thread your needle with green embroidery thread. Push the needle up through your pompom from the centre of the bottom of the speckled half and out through the top of the white half – leaving a tail at the bottom to secure later. Feed your needle tip firstly through the base of one leaf, then the loop on each of the three little bells and, finally, through the base of the second leaf.

5 Push the needle back down through the pompom from the top to the bottom, drawing it through carefully, but firmly, to secure the leaves and bells snugly into place at the top of the bauble.

6 Tie the two ends of the green embroidery thread firmly together and trim them so that the ends are lost in the pile of the speckled pompom yarn. Finally, tie the two white yarn ends together and trim neatly to create your hanging loop.

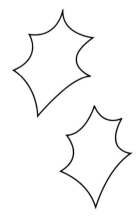

LEAF TEMPLATES (actual size)

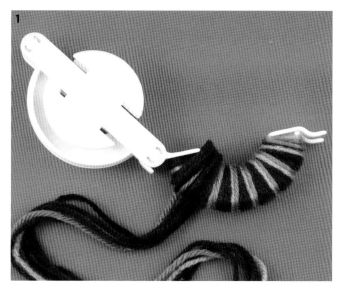

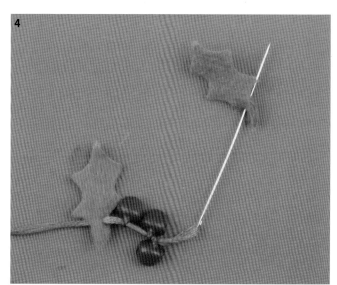

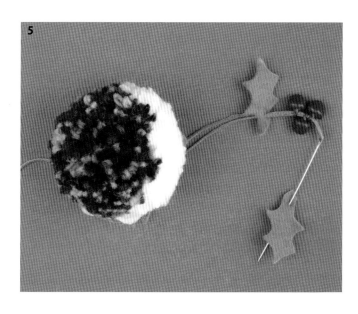

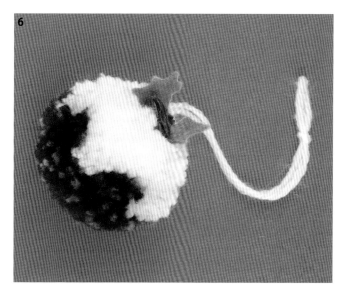

FELTED BAUBLES

These pompoms are turned into pretty baubles using felting techniques. The festive felted spheres are then decorated with glass beads and hung up using a traditional bauble fitting. You will need a washing machine and dryer to make these felted decorations.

YOU WILL NEED
For each bauble:
Oddments of deep red or pink chunky yarn, 100% wool
3⅜in (8.5cm) pompom maker
Small, sharp scissors
Sewing needle and strong cotton sewing thread (make sure your
    needle passes through the beads comfortably)
6in (15cm) square of nylon stocking fabric
Elastic band
Hanging fitting from an old or broken bauble
About 100 small glass beads
Soap, washing machine and dryer
Fabric glue

1 Make a red or pink pompom using a large pompom maker and thick yarn and tie firmly. Give the pompom a medium trim with sharp scissors.

2 Take the piece of nylon stocking and use it to wrap your pompom. Close it with an elastic band to make yourself a snugly, but not too firmly, encased pompom. Follow this process for as many pompoms as you like.

3 Set your washing machine to a hot wash and pop in all your parcelled pompoms. Add washing soap and use a hot wash (140°F/60°C) to felt your work. The addition of an old towel will enhance and encourage the felting process, but fabric softener will not help, so don't use any. When the washing machine cycle is complete, keep each bauble's wrapping on while you run them through a drying cycle in a dryer, or leave them somewhere well aerated to fully dry. Remove the elastic band to reveal your felted sphere.

Tip If you can't lay your hands on the hanging fitting from an old bauble, attach a simple loop using cotton embroidery thread at the end of step 7.

4 Thread your needle with strong sewing cotton and tie a knot in the end. Push the needle through your pompom to exit about 2in (5cm) from where it entered.

5 Draw your needle through and give it a firm tug, so that the knot at the end of the thread 'disappears' into the felt surface of the pompom. Thread one small bead on to the needle and reinsert, making sure that your needle passes through the bead comfortably. Reinsert the tip of the needle just next to where it had exited, and out again ⅜in (1cm) further on, thus anchoring the bead to the surface of the bauble.

6 Continue like this, threading one bead at a time onto your needle, reinserting the tip of the needle just next to where it exited, and out again ⅜in (1cm) further on. Steadily cover the surface of your felted sphere.

7 Remove the hanging fitting from an unwanted or broken bauble with a little tug. Apply fabric glue to its prongs.

8 Push the two prongs firmly into the felted surface of your bauble. Leave your work to one side for the glue to fully dry. You are now ready to hang your bauble on your tree.

1

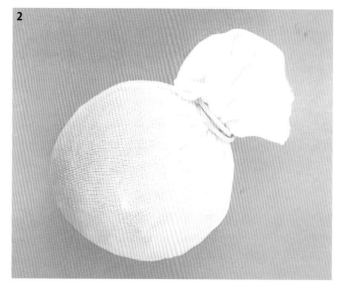

2

3

4

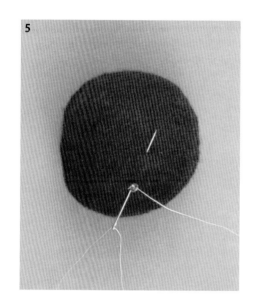

5

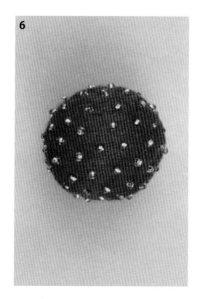

6

7

8

LITTLE DOVE

A traditional symbol of peace and hope, this cute pompom dove spins in the lightest breeze. Make a couple to hang together on your Christmas tree, or you could display one in a window or on a mantelshelf. In assorted colours, they would make pretty table decorations, too.

YOU WILL NEED
2½in (6.5cm) and 1⅜in (3.5cm) pompom
    makers
Oddments of white, pale blue and pink
    DK yarn and needle
Small, sharp scissors
Knitting needle (or similar blunt tool)
Fabric glue

1 To make the dove's body, take the larger pompom maker and wrap with white yarn to fill one half of it. Close this first half. On the second half, wrap pale blue yarn around the centre of the arches 25 times, overlapping the wraps.

2 Cut the pale blue yarn and then fill the remainder of the side with white yarn. Cut the white yarn, close the pompom maker and complete your pompom by tying it off with white yarn. Start trimming the pompom to shape, including the yarn used to tie the pompom. Do not trim the pale blue yarn at all at this point. Now part the two colours of yarn where they meet with your fingertips – and hold the pale blue yarn out of the way by shielding it with your fingers as you snip away. The blue yarn forms the base of the bird's tail. Refer to the bird template below to judge where you need to trim away at the tail and remove more yarn.

3 When you are satisfied with your trimming, make a few small snips to ensure that the ends of the blue yarn tufts are neat and even.

4 To make the bird's head, take the smaller pompom maker and fill one half with white yarn. Fill the second half with white yarn, leaving a small dip in the middle. Fill with 11–15 wraps of the pale blue yarn to finish this half.

5 Complete your pompom by tying it with pale blue yarn and giving it a hard trim, retaining the tie yarn ends. Use the end of a blunt tool, such as a knitting needle, to tweak the two blue yarn eye patches to make them as circular as you can.

6 Make a twisted cord (see page 117) with pale blue yarn. Slip the cord off the knitting needle and unravel it to achieve the length you want for the dove's beak – about ½in (1.5cm) – remembering that some of the beak's length will be lost in the pile of the pompom. Thread the yarn needle onto the two raw tail ends of the twisted cord (not the loop).

7 Push the needle through the small pompom at a position between the two eye patches. Bring the needle out at about 90° to the position it entered, at the point where you want the head to join the body. Repeat this with the loop end of the twisted cord. Tie a tight knot with the beak yarn ends so that it is buried within the pile of the pompom.

8 To add an eye, thread the needle with a short length of pink yarn and push it in through the centre of one blue eye patch and out again on the other side through the opposite eye patch. Trim both ends of the pink yarn flush with the surface of the pompom.

9 Join the head and the body by using two of the tail ends attached to the head. Working separately with each of the two yarns, thread them onto your needle and push the needle from the top of your pompom in the position where you want the head to sit, through to the other side. Do the same with the other tail end before tying them together in a firm knot, losing them in the pile, and trimming them flush with the surface.

10 Make a hanging loop with a length of pale blue yarn using a needle. Position it just behind the head on the bird's back. Start by pushing the needle up from the bottom, leaving a tail end of about 3in (7.5cm). Push the needle back down through the body pompom, just next to where it emerged, leaving a loop of about 3in (7.5cm). Tie the two ends off, snip the excess and give the loop a gentle tug to lose the knot in the pile of the pompom.

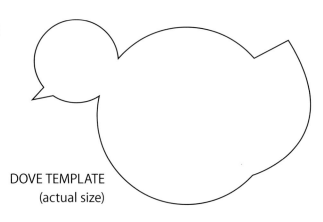

DOVE TEMPLATE
(actual size)

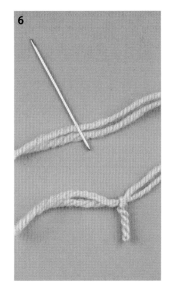

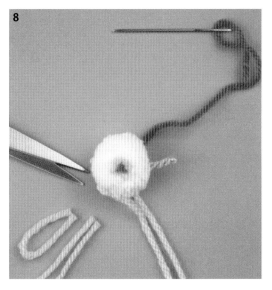

1

2

3

4

5

6

7

8

9

10

CHEERY SNOWMAN

This snowman is a jolly little character to hang from your tree. You can make larger or smaller snowmen too, just change the sizes of the pompom makers you use. You could add extra accessories of your own, such as a thin scrap of fabric to make a scarf.

YOU WILL NEED
2½in (6.5cm) and 1⅜in (3.5cm) pompom
    makers
Oddments of white, black, orange and
    blue DK yarn
Small, sharp scissors
Yarn needle
Knitting needle (or similar blunt tool)
D/3 (3.25mm) crochet hook
Tweezers (optional)

1 To make the body of the snowman, take the larger pompom maker and fill both sides with white yarn.

2 Complete the first pompom using white yarn to tie it. Give it a hard trim, including the tail ends. Put to one side.

3 Make the head by wrapping white yarn to fill the first side of your smaller pompom maker. Follow the chart below to wrap the second half with both white and black yarns. To do this, take small lengths – no more than 6in (15cm) – of black yarn to wrap around the arches to create coal teeth and eyes. The teeth take just two wraps, the eye four. Follow the chart for the positioning of these and don't worry if you go a bit wonky. This may take you a few goes, but remember that, once removed from the maker and trimmed, you can push and manipulate the black strands to more satisfying positions. When the second half is complete, close the maker and use sharp scissors to cut all the way around. At this point you will be able to see the features of the face appearing. Tie with a 16in (40cm) length of white yarn.

4 Give the head a hard trim, retaining the long tie tail ends.

5 If you want to make the eyes or teeth smaller, use your fingers or a pair of tweezers to pull single threads out. But be careful: while doing this hold the rest of the pompom firmly so that you only remove one strand of yarn at a time. Now tweak and tease the black yarns to manipulate them into a position you're happy with – two patches for eyes and a curve of dots for the mouth. Any accidental extra wraps of black yarn can be clipped short or removed with your fingers or tweezers and a sharp tug.

6 Now use the twisted cord method to make your snowman's 'carrot' nose with 20in (50cm) of orange yarn (see page 117). Unravel your cord to your required length – about ½in (1.5cm) – and tie a knot with the loop and the tail ends. Snip off the loop then thread the yarn needle onto the two raw tail ends of your twisted cord.

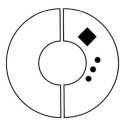

SNOWMAN'S HEAD CHART
◆ 4 wraps in black
• 2 wraps in black

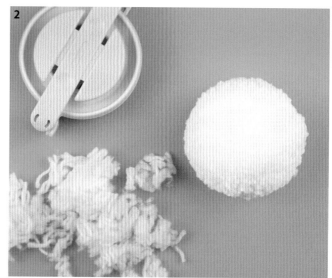

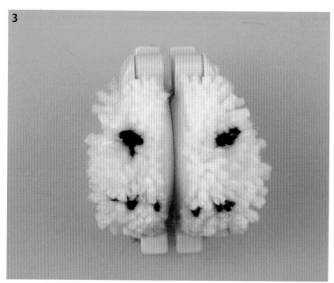

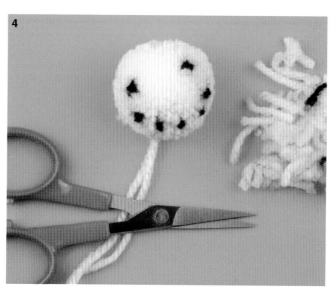

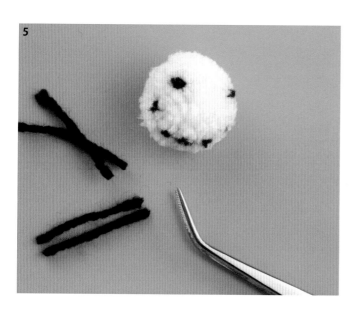

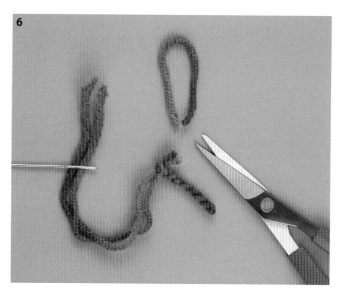

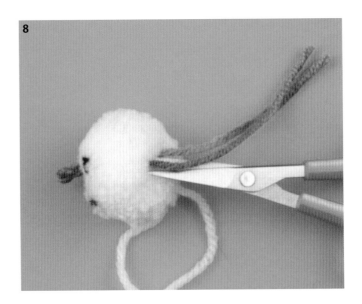

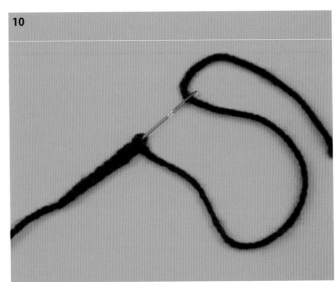

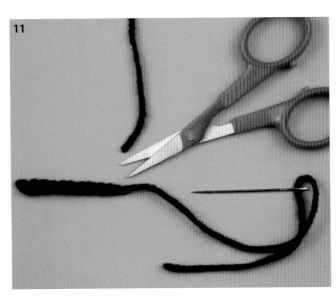

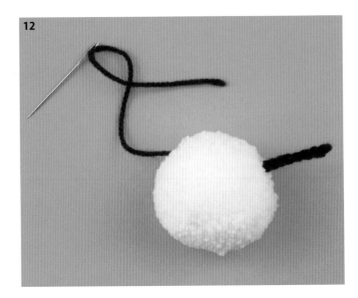

7 Push the needle through the small pompom at a position between the two eye patches and above the curve of mouth dots. Bring the needle out opposite the point where it entered. Repeat this with the other end of the twisted cord. Tie a tight knot with the nose yarn ends so that it is buried within the pile of the pompom.

8 Trim the tail ends of orange yarn carefully below the surface of the pompom to lose them in the pile.

9 Make a crochet chain of 10 for the arms (see Festive Ribbon, page 68, steps 4–5), starting with a slip knot 6in (15cm) from the end of your black yarn.

10 Pull the working tail of your yarn through the last chain and give it a little tug to secure it. Thread this tail end on to your needle and feed the needle back down through the chain you have just crocheted.

11 Pull the needle through, remove the needle and cut this tail end of yarn flush with the crocheted chain's surface.

12 Thread the remaining tail end onto the needle and push it through the body pompom in at the position you'd like one arm to sit.

13 Repeat from step 9 to 11 to make the second arm, positioning it on the other side of the snowman's body.

14 Re-thread one of the tail ends onto the needle and push it once more through to the other side so that it exits close by the other tail end. Tie the two tail ends together with a tight knot so that it is hidden deep within the pile of the yarn.

15 Trim the two tails of black yarn below the surface level of the pompom so that they are lost within the pile.

16 Join the head and body by threading the long white tail ends one at a time onto the needle and pushing the needle through from the top to the bottom of the body pompom.

17 Tie the tail ends together in a tight knot and trim flush with the surface of the pompom.

18 Finally, make the hanging loop. Take a 10in (25cm) length of blue yarn and thread one of the ends onto your needle. Push it from under the snowman's chin to exit out through the top of his head. Repeat with the other end and tie them together in a knot before trimming about ⅜in (1cm) from the knot to finish.

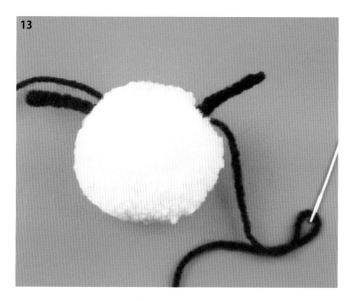

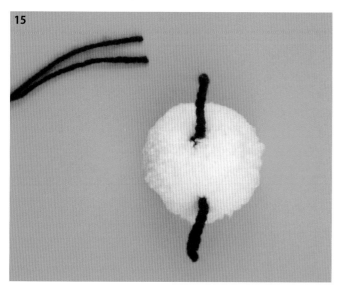

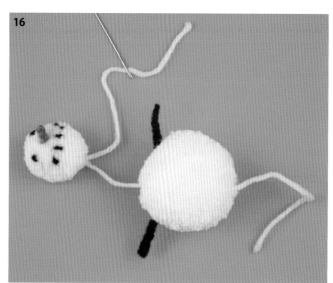

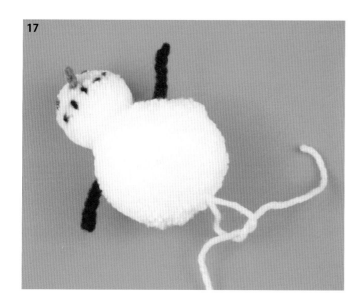

TWINKLING STAR

Make either a simple Christmas star to put at the top of your tree,
or smaller ones to hang from the tree branches or to spin in a window.
This is a sculpted piece – to turn your spherical, shaggy pompom into
a crisp little star you will need to give it a very heavy trim!

YOU WILL NEED
Oddments of yellow DK yarn
3⅜in (8.5cm) pompom maker
Small, sharp scissors
Yarn needle
2 large yellow buttons

1 Make your pompom using yellow yarn. Start trimming it, using Template 1 below to guide you. Pinch the pompom between your finger and thumb to flatten it, taking care to position the source of the tail ends in the centre of one of the sides.

2 You should end up with a flying saucer shaped pompom, the tail ends protruding from the centre of one of the flat sides. I've shown two pompoms here so that you can see the shape you're aiming for.

3 Take one of the tail ends and thread it onto the needle (ensuring first that the needle fits through the holes in your buttons). Feed the needle through one of the buttonholes from the back to the front, then again, through the other hole from front to back.

4 Now push the needle through the centre of the pompom disc to the other side and draw it through, pulling it firmly to secure the first button snugly against the surface of the disc. Repeat this process on the other side, finally pushing the needle back through to the first side again. Draw the needle out behind the first button, between it and the pile of the pompom's surface. Take the other tail end and tie the two of them together, pulling them firmly to tighten the knot snugly behind the button.

5 Trim off the tail ends flush with the edge of the button. Use the sharp scissors to start sculpting the star's shape. You can do this by eye, or by using Template 2 below.

6 When you are happy with your star and have checked both sides for symmetry, cut a length of yellow yarn 8in (20cm) long to make your hanging loop. Double it up, aligning the two ends, and thread the loop onto the needle. Insert the needle through the top of one of the star's points.

7 Draw the needle out on the opposite side, between two of the star's points. Pull the needle off, leaving the tail ends extending from one side of the star and the loop from the other. Tie a knot in the two tail ends and trim them to ⅜in (1cm).

8 Pull the loop gently so that the knotted end disappears into the pile of the yarn between the two points.

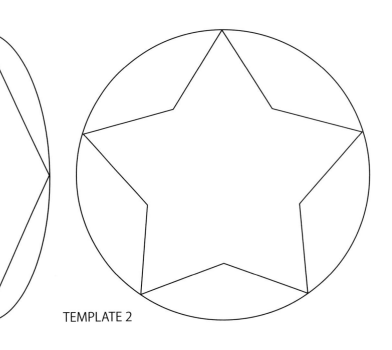

TEMPLATE 1

TEMPLATE 2

TINY FIR TREE

A traditional symbol of winter and celebrations, this little tree is a sculpted project made up from two pompoms. You can embellish it with tiny coloured beads fixed on with fabric glue, or with a small silver bell on the top and a bright, jingling string of fairy lights.

YOU WILL NEED
Oddments of green DK yarn
2½in (6.5cm) and 1⅝in (4.5cm)
    pompom makers
Green embroidery thread
Small, sharp scissors
Yarn needle
Fabric glue (optional)
¾in (2cm) button
⅜in (1cm) silver bell
30 x ¼in (6mm) coloured bells

1 Make your two pompoms, one about twice the size of the other. Take the largest of the two and flatten out one side of it, smoothing out the yarns of its pile and patting it down on your work surface. Now take up your scissors and trim the pompom to shape. You are looking to make a shape representing the bottom half of a cone. Use Template 1, below, as a guide. You can do more trimming later, so it's best to trim too little than too much at this stage. You can trim the tail ends off this part of your work.

2 Now start working on the smaller pompom. Flatten one side of it in the same way as you did with the other one – the opposite side to the tail ends. Trim away at it to create a small cone shape – this will be fitted on top of your larger piece from step 1. Retain the tail ends on this piece positioned at the narrow top of your cone. You can use Template 2, below, for guidance.

3 Hold the two halves of your tree up against one another to check the fit – it can be fairly rough at this point and be corrected with more trimming and sculpting later.

4 Thread one of the tail ends from your smaller pompom onto your yarn needle. Feed the needle down through the centre of the top to the centre of the flattened bottom and draw it through. Now push it through the larger pompom, down through the centre of the narrower end.

5 Draw the needle out through the centre of the flattened base of the larger pompom, push it through the back of the button to the front and draw it through. Now push the needle back down through the button's other hole, through both pompoms and out at the top of your tree. Give it a firm tug to pull the button snugly up against the base. You can introduce a bit of fabric glue between the two pompoms to make the join more permanent.

6 Tie the two tail ends together and trim them flush with the top of the tree. Take a length of green embroidery thread and thread it onto your needle. Push the needle in through the side of your work, about halfway up, and out through the top of it. Draw the needle through, leaving a tail end, and thread the silver bell onto it.

7 Feed the needle back through the loop in the bell again to hold it firmly, before pushing the needle back down through the top of the tree. Push and then draw the needle out near the thread's tail. Leave a loop at the top about 2in (5cm) long. Tie these two ends tightly together and trim them so that the knot gets lost in the pile of the tree.

8 Thread the needle again with a length of embroidery thread. One at a time, feed the coloured bells onto the thread and fix them roughly ⅜in (1cm) apart with knots. Knot the first one 4in (10cm) from the end of the thread.

9 Once all 30 bells are fixed on the thread, push the needle through the top of your tree, just beneath the silver bell.

10 Draw the needle through so that the first of the bells sits snugly against the top of the tree. Start wrapping your 'string of lights' around your tree. Use your needle and thread to anchor the bells as you go – every two or three bells, make a small stitch through your pompom to hold the thread between the bells to the surface of your tree.

11 To finish off, push the needle through to the other side of the tree and pull the needle off it, leaving the tail end. Thread the needle onto the remaining end of your string of lights. Push the needle through the tree to exit near the other tail end and pull the needle off. Tie these two ends firmly together, losing the knot within the pile of the pompom. Trim off the excess with sharp scissors. Finally, trim the base of your tree around the button so that this bottom surface is flush.

TEMPLATE 2
(actual size)

TEMPLATE 1
(actual size)

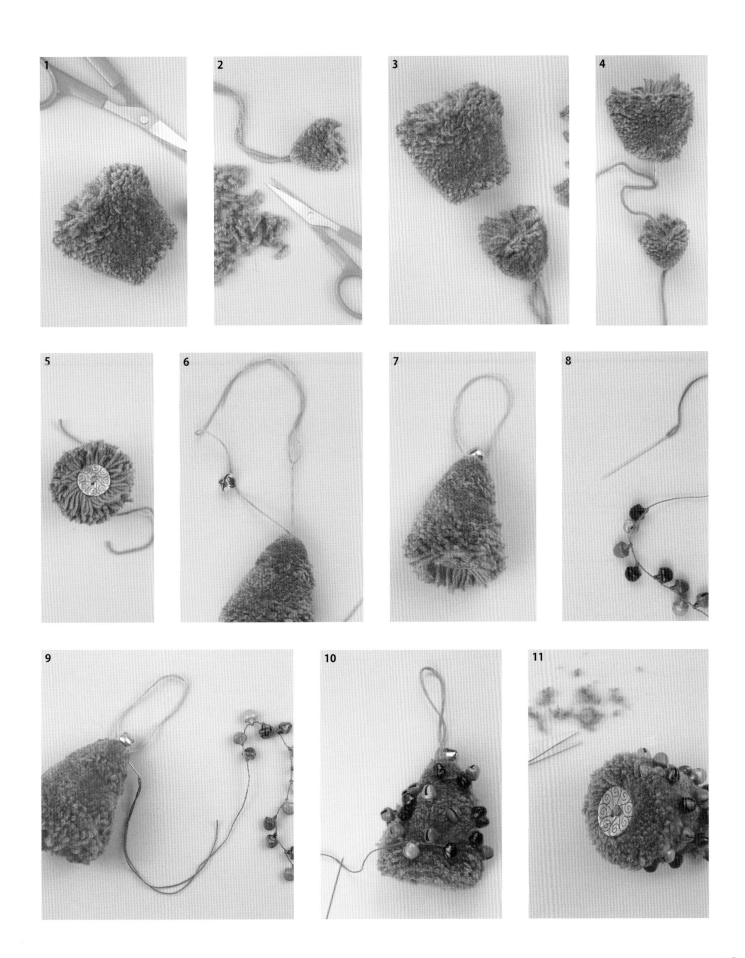

PENDANT DROP

Bring a touch of nostalgia to your home with this cheery decoration, reminiscent of glass drop baubles from the 1950s. Try making them in various tones of the same colour, or in clashing contrast colours, and hang them from your tree or in your windows to add a festive touch.

YOU WILL NEED
Oddments of DK yarn
2½in (6.5cm), 1⅝in (4.5cm) and 1⅜in (3.5cm)
    pompom makers
4 x contrasting beads
Cotton embroidery thread to match yarn
Embroidery needle
Small, sharp scissors

1 Fill each of your pompom makers with yarn. Cut and tie them firmly and give all three of your pompoms a hard trim, making them round and velvety.

2 Thread 18in (45cm) of embroidery thread onto the embroidery needle and tie a knot at the end. Push the needle through the centre of your largest pompom. Now thread one of the beads onto the thread.

3 Draw the needle all the way through, giving the thread a tug so that the knot at the end is pulled into and hidden by the pile of the pompom. Take the needle and push it back through the centre of the pompom, just next to the position it exited.

4 Pull the needle so that the bead sits snugly against the surface of the pompom, but does not get buried within it. Feed the needle through another of the beads. Now push the needle through the bead again, entering through the same side of the bead as you did before – the thread will be wrapped around the outside of the bead.

5 Use your fingers to push this bead along the embroidery thread and flush against the pompom so that the pompom now has a bead on either side. Thread the middle-sized pompom onto the thread now and push it down to sit next to the second bead. Now repeat step 4 with a third bead.

6 Use your fingers to push this third bead along the embroidery thread and flush against the second pompom. Thread the small pompom onto the thread and push it down to sit next to the third bead. Now feed a fourth and final bead onto the thread. Re-insert the needle into the pompom, just next to where the thread exited, and draw it out just next to the third bead.

7 Push the needle through the middle of the middle pompom, entering just next to the position of the existing thread and out just to one side of the second bead. Do the same, feeding the thread through the largest pompom and, this time, exiting through the middle of the first bead.

8 Push the needle back through the bead and out between it and the surface of the large pompom to create a hanging loop.

9 Now feed the needle back through the top of the bead, wrapping the thread around the outside of the bead, and out through one side of the large pompom.

10 Use sharp scissors to cut the tail end of your thread flush with the surface of the pompom.

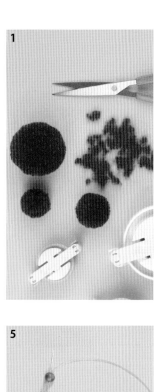

1

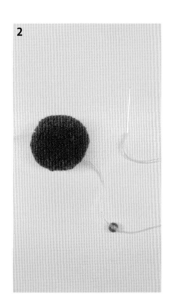

2

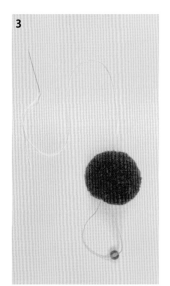

3

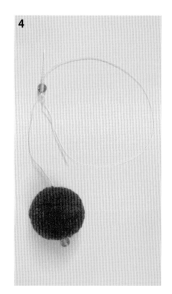

4

5

7

8

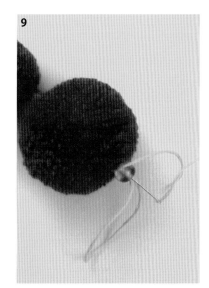

9

10

GIFTS & WRAPPING

JINGLE BELLS RIBBON

Add an extra bit of luxury to a special gift by making this cheerful ribbon. It's a great way to use up ribbon scraps, too. The pompoms and bells are added just to the part of the ribbon that goes along the top and down the sides of your wrapped parcel, so that the bottom sits flat.

YOU WILL NEED
Oddments of dark pink DK yarn
1in (2.5cm) pompom maker
1in (2.5cm) wide white cotton tape (for quantities see step 1)
½in (1.5cm) wide red grosgrain tape (for quantities see step 1)
Small, sharp scissors
Yarn needle
Pen
Ball of string
Sewing machine
Red and white thread
Sewing needle and pins
Iron
¼in (6mm) silver bells

1 To work out how much ribbon you will need, take a ball of string and tie it around the parcel. Tie a bow at the top and trim both ends to your desired length. Before removing the string, mark a point halfway down each side (as shown in the diagram below) and again 1in (2.5cm) either side of the base of the bow. Now take this string off and you have created a template for your ribbon. Cut the red and white tape to the length of your string template plus 3in (7.5cm). Lay the red tape along the centre of the white tape, with raw short ends aligned, and pin in place.

2 Using red as the top thread in your sewing machine and white in the bobbin, topstitch along each side of the red ribbon, just a fraction in from the two long edges, to stitch the two together. Turn the tape over and fold each short end in by ½in (1.25cm) and press with a hot iron.

3 Now fold each of the short ends over again at 45°, press again and pin in position.

4 Thread your needle with white thread and stitch down the ribbon along its 45° fold at both ends of your work.

5 Turning your ribbon over, you should now have a white ribbon with a red stripe down the middle and two sharp-angled ends.

6 Make your little pompoms, giving them a hard trim and retaining their two tail ends. I needed 10 in all to cover the two 8in (20cm) long areas from my string template.

Making a template

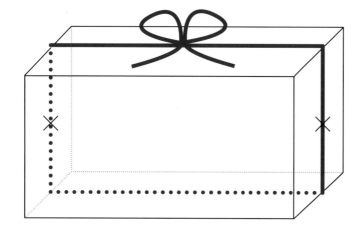

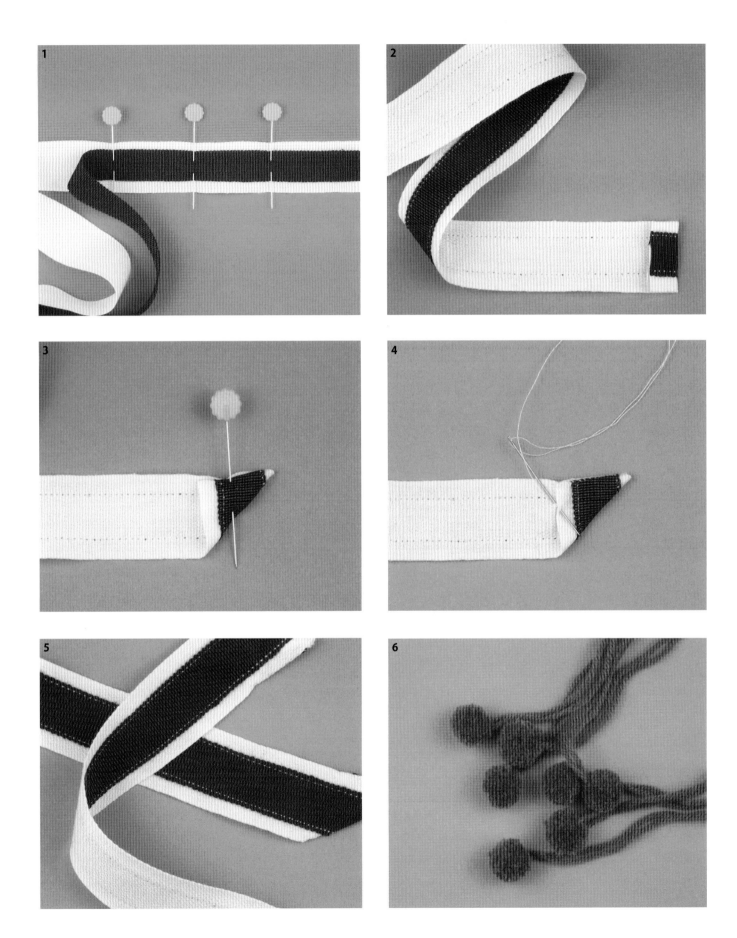

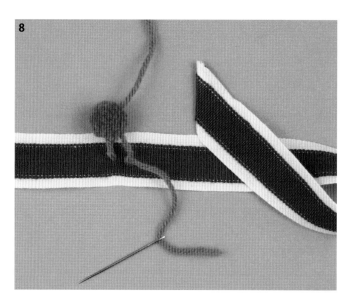

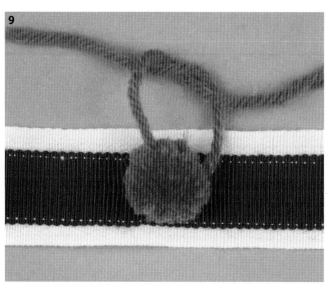

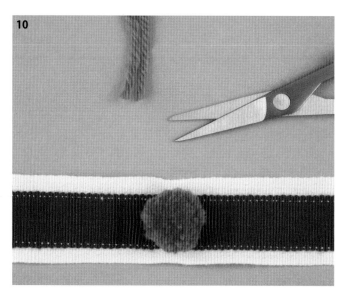

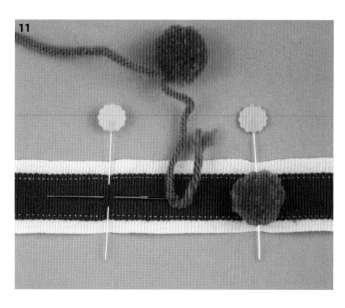

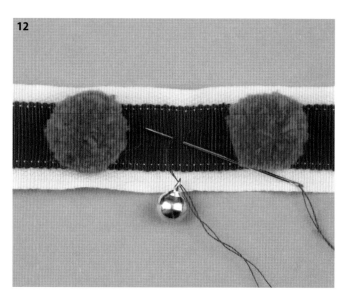

7 Take one pompom and thread the yarn needle onto one of its tail ends. Start at the first template marker from one angled end and make a ¼in (6mm) stitch at this point, in the centre of the red ribbon and running between the red ribbon and the white tape so that no stitching shows on the other side. Draw the needle through.

8 Repeat this procedure with the other tail end, entering where the first exited and exiting where the first entered.

9 Tie the two tail ends firmly together. Your pompom should be sitting securely and snugly against the red ribbon.

10 Now trim the two ends so they are lost in the pile of the pompom.

11 Continue attaching your pompoms to the ribbon until you reach the next marker on the string template. Space your pompoms out evenly, marking their positions with pins in the first instance and placing them roughly 2in (5cm) apart.

12 Finally, stitch on silver bells between your pompoms for a little extra Christmas cheer. You will need two fewer bells than the number of pompoms you have used. Use red thread and run your needle between the red ribbon and the white tape to keep the stitching hidden.

JOLLY HOLLY

Holly sprigs are an iconic symbol of Christmas. Made out of felt with little pompoms for berries, these decorations are just perfect for the dining table, to add to a gift or even to wear as a Christmas corsage.

YOU WILL NEED
Oddments of red and orange DK yarns
1in (2.5cm) pompom maker
Small, sharp scissors
Light and dark green felt
Florist's wire
Florist's tape
Fabric glue

NOTE
Florist's tape is made from stretchy crêpe paper. It is also slightly waxed and therefore sticks to itself when bound tightly around wire.

1 Make a bundle of pompom berries using the red and orange yarns. Give them a hard trim and retain their tail ends.

2 Cut out a leaf in the lighter green felt, using one of the templates below. Cut a 6in (15cm) length of florist's wire and fold one end over by about ¾in (2cm) and bend it to curve along the spine of the leaf. Now lay your felt leaf on top of the dark green felt to check that it fits.

3 Lift the light green leaf and wire and apply fabric glue to the reverse of the cut-out leaf. Lay the wire along it and then lay it glue-side down on to the dark green felt, sandwiching the wire between the two layers. Press the light green leaf down onto the wire and darker felt with your thumb to ensure every bit of it is glued down and leave to dry. Cut away any excess dark green felt, following the contours of the light green leaf.

4 You will be left with a felt holly leaf with a wire stem. Make two more similar leaves in the same way.

5 Bunch the three leaves together, flipping one over to vary the greens, and twist their stems together to keep them in position.

6 Place a bundle of pompom red and orange berries at their bases, nestled at the top of the wire stems. Use the florist's tape to bind the tail ends of the pompoms firmly to the wire stems.

7 After a few wraps, give the tail ends a tug to make sure they're firmly held against the base of the leaves, and trim them down to about 2½in (6.5cm).

8 As you near the bottom of the stems, bend the wire up over itself to avoid any sharp ends before completing the binding.

LEAF
TEMPLATES
(actual size)

1

2

3

4

5

6

7

8

MISTLETOE SPRIG

Traditionally hung as a decoration at Christmas, mistletoe adds rustic romance to the festivities. This cute pompom version of a sprig of mistletoe can be used to embellish a gift, hung on your Christmas tree, or can be cheekily pinned to the side of a hat!

YOU WILL NEED
Oddments of cream, white, pale and mid green DK yarns
1in (2.5cm) pompom maker
Small, sharp scissors
Yarn needle
Florist's wire
Florist's tape

NOTE
Florist's tape is made from stretchy crêpe paper. It is also slightly waxed and therefore sticks to itself when bound tightly around wire.

1 To make the leaves, you need the mid green yarn, florist's wire and tape. Cut a 7in (18cm) length of florist's wire and bend it in half from its middle. Do not pinch or press the bend, but keep its natural curve. Cut a 1 yard (1m) length of yarn. Take the end of the yarn and lay it on the wire so that one end of it lines up with the two ends of the wire.

2 Bind the ends of the wire and yarn with the tape. Start by covering the ends, then start binding up tightly to hold the yarn and wire together to a point about 1½in (4cm) from the tip. Cut the tape and pinch and press this end against the wound tape to make sure it's firmly adhered. Thread the needle onto the yarn and start 'weaving' your leaf. Push the needle from the right to the left, through the wire loop from the front and out from under the left-hand wire.

3 Draw the needle and yarn through to the left. Now insert the needle through the front of the wire loop again, from the left to the right. Draw the needle through and tug gently to keep the tension firm. Continue weaving the yarn from right to left and left to right, gradually filling the loop of the wire.

Tip For a decoration to hang on your front door, make a bunch of sprigs and attach to a twig using florist's tape. See Berry Branches (page 80) for the technique.

4 As you reach the top of the leaf, keep the tip of your finger at the apex of the bend in the wire to keep the 'stitches' in place until you have completely filled the leaf with woven yarn. Now push the needle tip vertically through the centre of the yarn leaf from the curved top, ensuring that it is running through the yarn and not visible on either side of the leaf.

5 Push the tip of the needle out about 1in (2.5cm) down from the top of the leaf and draw it and the yarn through. Snip off the tail end of the yarn flush to the surface of the leaf using small, sharp scissors. Make a second leaf, following the instructions from step 1–5 again.

6 Make the mistletoe berries. Use your small pompom maker to make two or three small pompoms. Give them a hard trim to make small, tight little berries, retaining their ties for attaching them to their leaves.

7 Place the two leaves next to each other, aligning their bottom tips and pinching their stems together so that the florist's tape holds them temporarily in place. Bunch the berries' ties together and position the berries themselves about 1½in (4cm) from the bottom of the leaves. Starting snugly up against the berries where their ties join them, wrap florist's tape firmly around the ties and the leaf stems to join them altogether. As you reach about ⅜in (1cm) from the end, snip off the excess yarn with the small scissors before finishing the tape wrapping and completing your mistletoe.

1

2

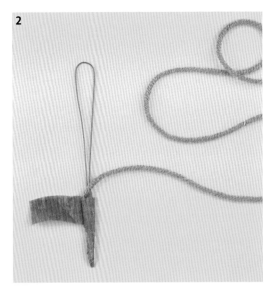

3

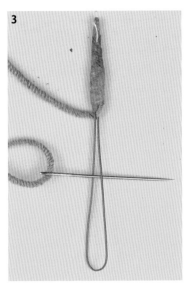

4

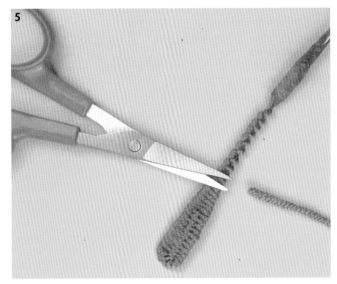

5

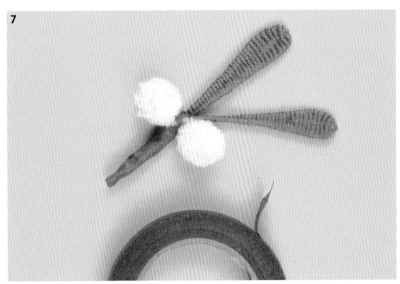

6

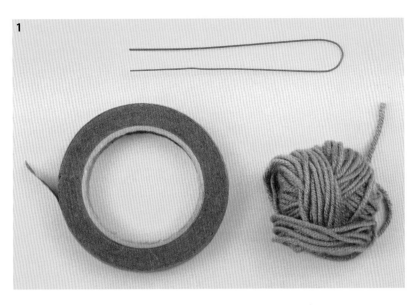

7

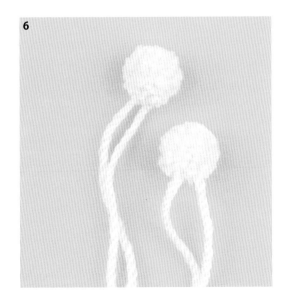

CHRISTMAS STOCKING

By adding a hand-made festive trim to a stocking you can create infinite variations for family members as special heirloom gifts. If you're short of time, embellish an existing stocking or even a chunky-knit walking sock with a pompom trim by simply starting at step 10.

YOU WILL NEED
For the pompom trim:
Oddments of antique gold/yellow DK yarn
   (or your choice of colour)
¾in (2cm) pompom maker
Small, sharp scissors
Yarn needle

For the stocking:
20 x 22in (50 x 55cm) gingham or fabric of
   your choice for the outer and hanging loop
17 x 22in (43 x 55cm) white fabric for lining
A blunt tool such as a knitting needle
Sewing machine and thread
Pins
Pen or fabric marker
Iron

Tip Make stockings for every member of your family, varying the colour of the fabric or the pompoms for each person.

1 Make a hanging loop from a piece of fabric measuring 6 x 1½in (10 x 4cm). With the fabric wrong side down (if you are using gingham, there won't be a right and wrong side) and fold in half to align the two long edges. Pin or tack along this edge, before stitching a ¾in (1cm) seam along it.

2 Turn the tube of fabric right-side out using your knitting needle and give it a good press.

3 Topstitch along both long sides about 1/16in (3mm) in from the edges. Use the stocking template on page 65 to cut all your other fabric pieces.

4 Place two main pieces – one outer and one lining – right sides together and align their top edges. Pin or tack before stitching a ⅜in (1cm) seam here. Press this seam open with a hot iron. Do the same with the second lining and outer pieces. (Unless using gingham or white, it is important that you join the lining and outer fabrics as mirror images to make a back and front for your stocking).

5 Place the two pieces of your work right sides together and align all their raw edges. Start pinning or tacking all the way around, incorporating the folded hanging loop between the two pieces of lining, as indicated on the template. Make sure the folded end of the loop lies towards the middle of the fabric and the raw short ends aligning the raw edge. You also need to leave a 3in (7.5cm) turning gap, also indicated on the template.

6 Stitch a ⅜in (1cm) seam around the edge of your stocking. Reverse stitch at either side of the turning gap and also over the hanging loop for extra strength. Trim the seam allowance to 3/16in (5mm) all the way around apart from at the turning gap. Cut little Vs at the top of the foot, and snip into the seam allowance at the toe and heel of the outer and the opposite for the lining (Vs at the toe and heel, snips at the top of the foot) to make the shaping as smooth as possible when turned out.

7 Press the seams open as best you can, taking great care with the iron. Carefully turn your stocking right side out through the turning gap.

1

2

3

4

5

6

7

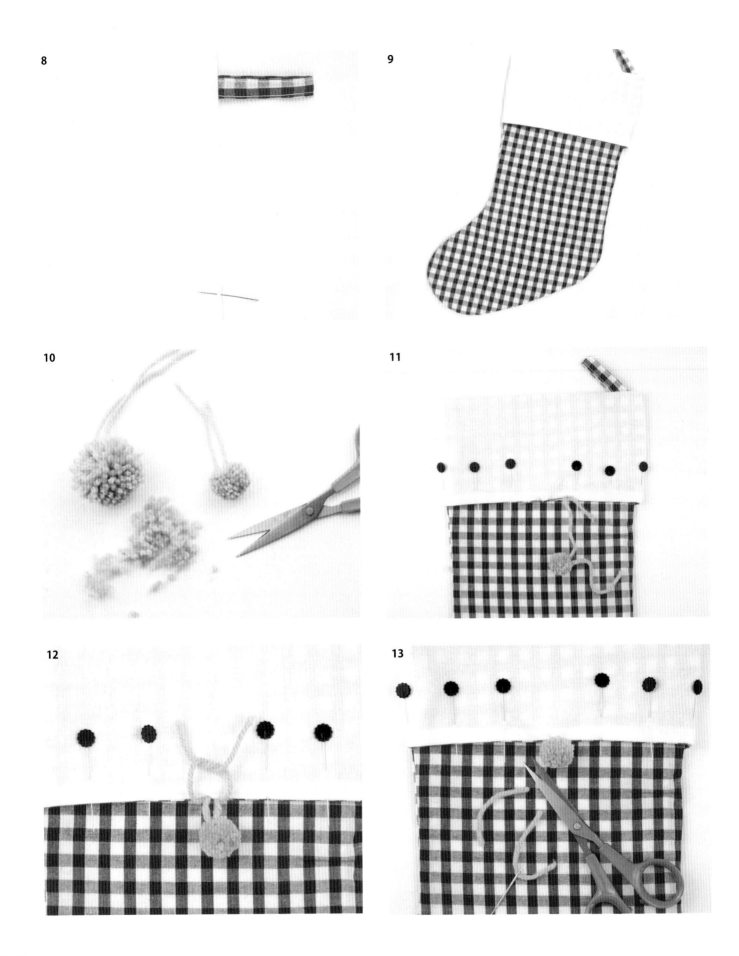

8

9

10

11

12

13

8 Fold in the raw edges at the turning gap and then close it by hand using small overstitches.

9 Push the lining down inside the gingham outer and tweak the seams between your fingers to make them as sharp as you can. Fold the top over to make a cuff and give the whole sock a good press.

10 Make your pompoms. You will need 12 for the stocking. Give them a hard trim to leave them with a velvety surface, while retaining the tail ends for attaching to the stocking cuff.

11 Use pins to mark the positions for each of your pompoms, distributing them equally around the cuff edge. Stitch your pompoms on in the marked positions. Thread one tail end onto your needle. Push the needle through the edge of the cuff seam, where the two fabrics meet, and out again just ⅛in (5mm) further on.

12 Thread the second tail onto the needle and push it through the other way – in where the previous tail exited and out through the point where it entered. Tie the two ends together in a tight knot.

13 Thread the tails, together or one at a time, back onto the needle, then push the needle through the centre of the pompom. Remove the needle and trim the tail ends flush with the pompom's surface using sharp scissors. Repeat steps 11–13 to attach all the pompoms.

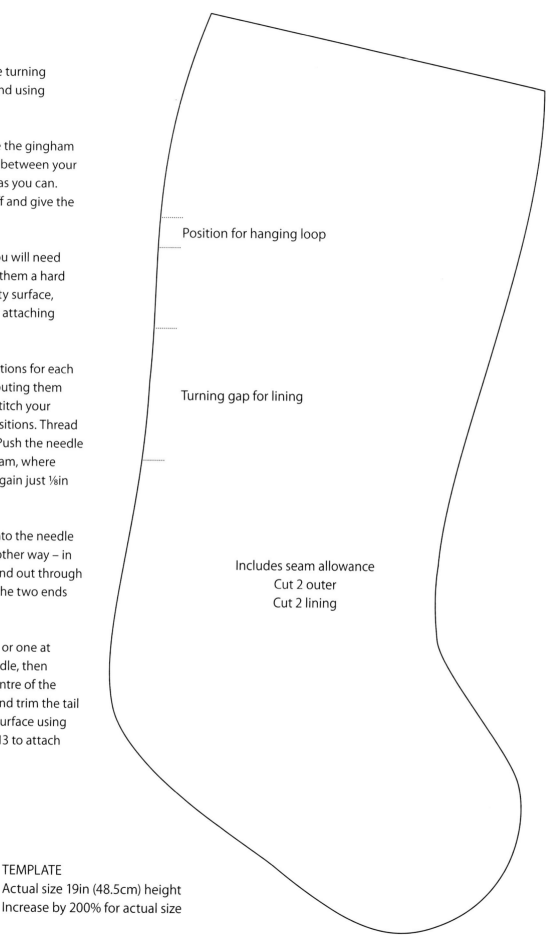

Position for hanging loop

Turning gap for lining

Includes seam allowance
Cut 2 outer
Cut 2 lining

TEMPLATE
Actual size 19in (48.5cm) height
Increase by 200% for actual size

FESTIVE RIBBON

Make a crochet ribbon, finished off at both ends with a soft pompom, to be used again and again. Make this project in different sizes and colours to match your wrapping and decorations. Or you can cluster four or five small pompoms at either end in place of the single large ones.

YOU WILL NEED
Oddments of DK yarn
2½in (6.5cm) pompom maker
Small, sharp scissors
Yarn needle
E/4 (3.5mm) crochet hook

1 Fill both sides of the pompom maker with your choice of yarn.

2 Cut all around the edge of your pompom maker with sharp scissors.

3 Tie off with yarn directly from your ball of wool – do not cut it to length. Remove carefully from the pompom maker. Use the sharp scissors to trim your ball – a medium trim will give a lovely soft, bouncy quality. Take care to keep the ball attached to the yarn from your ball of wool – you can cut the shorter tie tail end flush with the surface of your pompom ball, leaving the yarn coming directly from the ball of wool remaining.

4 Using the attached yarn, start to crochet your 'ribbon'. Use the crochet hook to make an initial slip knot (or chain) by making a loop and pulling another loop, made with the free end, through it.

5 Continue to chain until you have a 'ribbon' to the length you desire. Trim the yarn to 8in (20cm) and pull it through the last chain to finish.

6 Make another pompom following steps 1 and 2, but this time trimming one tail end to about 8in (20cm) and the other one flush as you trim the ball. Thread the tail end at the end of your crochet chain onto the yarn needle and feed it through your second pompom. You need to position the needle so that it draws out close to the tail end left on this second pompom.

7 Taking your two tail ends from step 6, tie them firmly into a tight knot to secure them to your crocheted chain.

8 Trim the two tail ends flush with the surface of the second pompom and you're ready to tie it around a parcel.

Tip Use white yarn and your pompoms become snowballs! Or try using mixed yarns for this project to use up any scraps you have lying around.

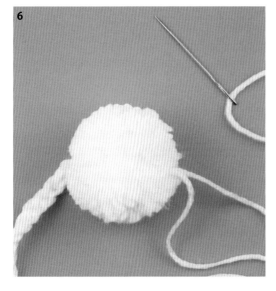

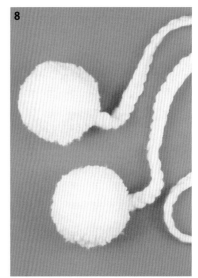

AROUND
THE HOUSE

CANDLE CROWN

Add a little seasonal embellishment to your dining table or mantelshelf over Christmas with this pretty candle holder. Mix red and white yarns to create light and dark speckled pompoms – you could vary the sizes of your pompoms to add more variety, too.

YOU WILL NEED
White and red 100% wool DK yarns
2½in (6.5cm) pompom maker
12in (30cm) of ¹/₃₂in (1mm) thick red elastic
Shallow food tin to fit your candle
White paint suitable for a metal surface
Paintbrush
Large darning needle
Small, sharp scissors
Pillar candle

1 Make all your pompoms. Use the pompom maker and vary the tones of the speckled pompoms by using different proportions of the red and white yarns. For the darkest pompom bind the pompom maker's arches with two red and one white (2:1) yarn at the same time. Doing this also means you can make pompoms much more quickly!

2 Complete the first pompom by cutting and then tying it with a length of yarn. Snip off the yarn tail ends and give your pompom a hard trim to leave it with a velvety, speckled surface.

3 Continue by making more pompoms. For increasingly lighter versions use 1:1, 1:2 and 1:3 proportions of red to white yarn. By all means experiment and mix it up to make your own unique design. I needed to make eight pompoms to decorate this candle holder, but you may need more or fewer pompoms for your own.

4 Thread a length of your elastic onto your large-eyed needle to use as a string to hold all the pompoms together. Push the needle through the centre of one of your pompoms, holding the ball firmly within your fist and gently tug the needle to draw it through – you want to avoid destroying the tightness of the pompom by pulling yarn out of it along with the needle and elastic.

5 Continue threading the pompoms until they are all on the elastic.

6 Make sure the tin you have chosen is wide enough to accommodate the candle. Give the outside of the tin a couple of coats of paint, leaving enough time between each layer for the paint to dry fully.

7 Tie a knot in the two tail ends of the elastic, testing the tension you create in the elastic around the tin to ensure a snug fit. Make sure your knot is very secure by giving the tail ends a very firm pull, before trimming them to about ⅜in (1cm). Position the bracelet of pompoms around your tin.

8 Now add your candle to complete your seasonal decoration. This project can be made using various sizes of candles and tins, which will then look wonderful clustered together to make a table centrepiece.

Tip Make sure that you use 100% wool yarn, which contains a natural fire retardant. This makes it safer to use near a naked flame than artificial fibre. Having said that, don't leave candles unattended, do not let them burn too low and ensure that your tin is taller than the height of your pompoms.

1

2

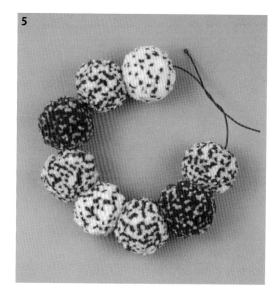

3

4

5

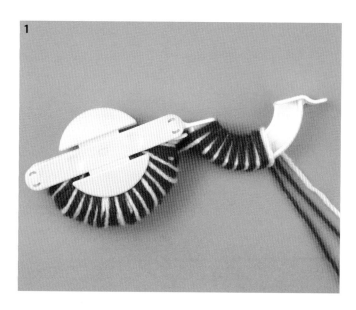

6

7

8

WINTER WREATH

Symbolizing eternality – with no beginning or end – the wreath has become a familiar Christmas decoration. This version, made from a luxurious pile of clustered pompoms, can be hung in a window or on a mantelshelf. The colour palette and size of your wreath is completely up to you, and you can add bells or glass baubles for extra sparkle.

YOU WILL NEED
A variety of oddments of green DK yarns (you can use
    a limited palette or a kaleidoscopic mix)
White DK yarn for berries
Assorted pompom makers: 3⅜in (8.5cm), 2½in (6.5cm),
    1⅝in (4.5cm), 1⅜in (3.5cm) and 1in (2.5cm)
60in (150cm) small dark green pompom trim
6 small vintage glass decorations (optional)
Yarn needle
10½ x 10½in (27 x 27cm) thick card
Craft knife and cutting mat
Pencil and a pair of compasses
Fabric glue
Bradawl or large, sharp yarn needle
Sharp scissors

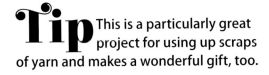
Tip This is a particularly great project for using up scraps of yarn and makes a wonderful gift, too.

1 Start off by making all your green pompoms. I made: 4 x 3⅜in (8.5cm), 10 x 2½in (6.5cm), 10 x 1⅝in (4.5cm), 10 x 1⅜in (3.5cm), 6 x 1in (2.5cm). When you give them a medium to hard trim, retain their tie tails for fixing them onto your card later. Take your card and draw a 10in (25.5cm) circle on to it using your compasses. Positioning the pin of your compass in exactly the same place again, now draw a 6½in (16.5cm) circle. Use a craft knife and mat to cut out your wreath 'doughnut'. Use your fabric glue to stick the tiny pompom trim around the outside and inside cut edges of the card. Place it so that the pompoms extend over the card's edge. Leave to dry. This is the front of your card base.

2 Make your hanging loop. Push the blade of your craft knife through the card roughly ½in (1.25cm) below the edge and horizontally to it. Make the two slots wide enough to fit your ribbon.

3 From the front of your wreath take 8in (20cm) of ribbon and fold it in half. Use the blunt edge of the blade to push the loop of the ribbon through the cut slot. Turn your work over and draw it through to make a loop, leaving about ½in (1.25cm) of the two raw ends at the front of your work. Turn the card back over again and glue the tail ends of the ribbon down onto the card with fabric glue. Leave to dry.

4 Take a bradawl or large needle and pierce a pair of holes about ¼in (5–7mm) apart in your card base.

5 Lay the green pompoms down in front of you and take a bit of time to arrange them on the front of your card base to decide what order to fix them in. When you are happy with their colour and size distribution, take a photograph to refer to as you continue to work. Affix your first pompom to the card. Thread each yarn tail end onto your yarn needle and then through from the front to the back of your card base, each pompom's tail ends through one of the pierced holes.

6 Turn the work over and tie your tail ends together in a firm knot against the surface of the card. Trim with sharp scissors.

7 Continue adding pompoms and tying them at the back.

8 Try to cover your card base completely – this may involve you making a few last minute small pompoms to fill any annoying little spaces.

9 Using the white yarn, make six small pompoms using the 1in (2.5cm) pompom maker and give them a hard trim, retaining their tail ends. Starting just below the hanging loop, fix them around your wreath at equal distances, tying them into position using the same technique as before with a pair of pierced holes.

10 If you like, tie little vintage glass decorations to each of the small white pompoms, wrapping the hanging string under the pompom, around its tail ends.

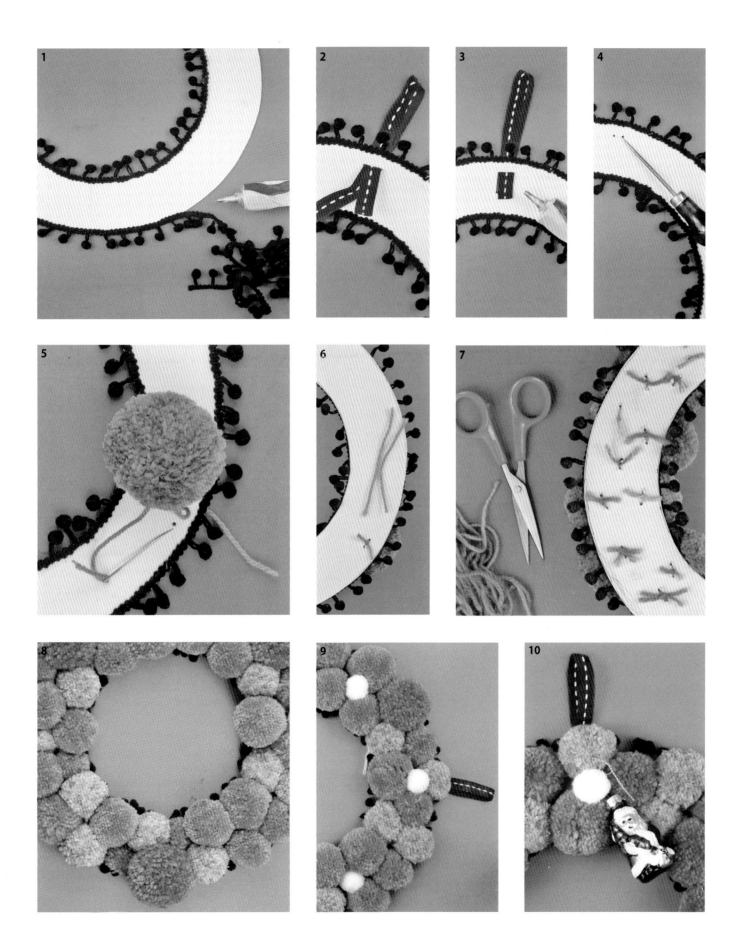

BERRY BRANCHES

Bring a little bit of the outside into your home for the festive season. These berry branches are made using scraps of red yarn but you could use any colour you like to coordinate with other decorations, or use a glittery yarn to add a sparkle. Variegated yarns add extra visual texture. Stand them in a vase, or lay them along a table.

YOU WILL NEED
Oddments of red DK yarn
1in (2.5cm) pompom maker
Small, sharp scissors
Fabric glue
Florist's tape
Twigs

5 A little distance below, add a couple more berries. Attach them in the same way, using 6in (15cm) strips of tape, pressing the beginning and finishing ends down firmly; the warmth of your fingers and thumbs will help the wax to adhere the ends as you wrap your way down the twig.

6 Add one more pair of berries. Continue wrapping the twig with tape.

7 Use your fingers and thumbs to smooth the tape down over and bumps and nobbles in order to retain the character of the twig's surface.

8 Make as many twigs as you like, varying their length slightly and also the distances between the groups of berries for a more natural effect.

1 Firstly, make some berries. Fill your pompom maker with red yarn.

2 Close your pompom maker and use sharp scissors to cut all the way around before tying as firmly as you can with red yarn. Release the pompom from the maker and give it a hard trim. Retain the tail ends and cut them to about 2in (5cm) in length.

3 Continue making berries following steps 1 and 2. Assemble your materials: pompom berries, twig, scissors, florist's tape, ready to start attaching the berries. Add an average of seven berries to each twig.

4 Place the first berry at the top of your twig with its tail ends lying along it. Use a 6in (15cm) strip of your florist's tape to bind around the twig and the tail ends. After a couple of wraps, give the tail ends a little tug to ensure that the berry sits snugly against the top of the twig.

Tip You could use strips of masking tape in place of the florist's tape. Cut the strips to a width of ³⁄₈in (1cm). You will end up with cream-coloured twigs, which look great with red, green or cream berries.

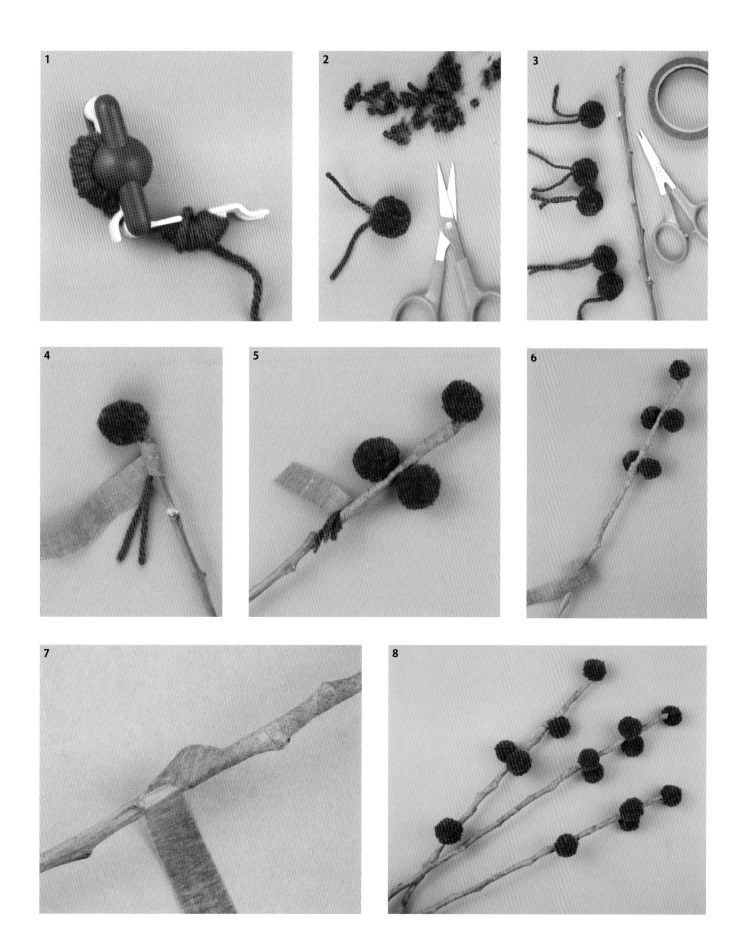

SNOWY TREE

A bold Christmas accessory to enhance and adorn any festive table or windowsill. This pompom tree combines traditional seasonal charm with hand-crafted character, and the graduated colour of the pompoms gives a magical snow-dusted effect.

YOU WILL NEED
Oddments of white and green DK yarns
1⅝in (4.5cm) pompom maker
14 x 14in (35 x 35cm) of white card
14 x 14in (35 x 35cm) of green paper
12in (30cm) of household string, or a pair
    of compasses, and a pencil
Adhesive putty
⅜in (1cm) wide double-sided tape
Sticky tape (optional)
Small, sharp scissors
Paper scissors
Glue gun
30–35 small ¾in (2cm) diameter baubles
2 x 2½in (6cm) squares of silver craft card
Wooden skewer
Scalpel
Glue
5 x sewing clips or paper clips

1 Make your pompoms – you will need a deceptively large number so do them in batches, but you don't have to have them all ready before you start constructing the tree. You will need plain white pompoms through to solid green ones. You can make speckled ones from different proportions of white and green yarn in between. Make the speckled ones by wrapping the pompom maker with several strands at once. This tree is made up of 9 x solid white, 20 x 2:1 white/green, 16 x 1:1 white/green, 16 x 1:2 white/green and 45 x solid green pompoms.

2 Tie and remove each pompom from the pompom maker, and give it a hard trim using sharp scissors and cutting off the tail ends.

3 As you progress you will be building up the various tones of green and white pompoms needed for the tree. Set one white pompom aside to use later at step 11.

4 Take your pencil and tie one end of your string to it, near the drawing end. Tie a knot in the other end and press it into the adhesive putty. Draw a line ⅜in (1cm) in from one edge of your white card. Press the adhesive putty with the knot of string into a position in the corner of the card. Pressing with a finger on the knot and tack to make sure it stays in place, hold the pencil at 90° to the surface of the card and draw an arc from one side of the corner of the card to the other. Alternatively, use a pair of compasses.

5 Cut along the curved line with paper scissors. Repeat this process from step 4 with the green paper. Now tie another knot in your string 5in (12.5cm) from the pencil. Press this knot into the tack and again, position it in the corner of your paper, then use the pencil to draw an arc. Cut along this line and then glue it to the bottom part of your card, aligning the edges. Snip ⅜in (1cm) off the right-angled corner. Run double-sided tape down one side of your paper/card, aligning with the pencil line you drew in step 3.

6 Peel the backing paper from the tape and roll your card into a cone, overlapping the two straight edges and sticking them together. If necessary, run a strip of sticky tape along this join for extra strength.

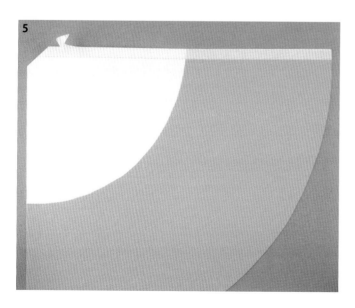

7

8

9

10

11

12

7 Arrange the pompoms in tonal groups. Following the manufacturer's instructions, use the glue gun to stick your pompoms to the prepared cone, starting at the top with the lightest and working through to the darkest for the lower part of your tree.

8 When they are all attached, trim the bottom of the card cone flush with the last layer of pompoms.

9 Remove the metal hangers from your little baubles and use your glue gun to apply glue around the top of the open stem.

10 Push the glued end of the bauble deep in amongst and between the pompoms, ensuring that it makes contact with the card cone beneath. Hold it firmly in position for a few minutes whilst the glue goes off a bit. You can do this with your other hand slipped inside the cone to apply pressure from within, too. Continue adding baubles in this way. You can plan where they go, or simply add them at random.

11 Use the star template (see right) to cut a star from your silver card. Push the single remaining white pompom onto your skewer. Lay the remaining square of silver card right side down and spread glue over the wrong side of it.

12 Lay the tip of the skewer on the glued card, and place the cut star wrong side down on top of it. Press the two layers of card together and hold in position with sewing or paper clips. When dry, use paper scissors or a scalpel to cut the excess card away to leave you with a double-sided star on the end of the skewer. Push the white pompom up to sit snugly under the star. Slot the skewer down into the small hole at the top of your cone to finish off the top of your tree.

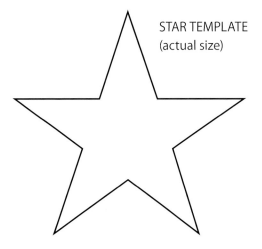

STAR TEMPLATE
(actual size)

Tip An alternative idea would be to use multicoloured pompoms in place of the baubles at step 10.

BUTTON CARD PEGS

Displaying cards takes up space, but if you hang a length of string or ribbon against a wall, you can simply pin your seasonal cards to it with these cute little pompom pegs. There's nothing to stop you using limitless colours of paint, yarn and buttons, and even using various sizes of pompom balls!

YOU WILL NEED
For each peg:
Oddments of white DK yarn
1⅜in (3.5cm) pompom maker
Small, sharp scissors
Yarn needle
Wooden clothes peg
Acrylic paint
Paintbrush
All-purpose glue
1in (2.5cm) button

1 Take the clothes peg apart, separating the two wooden bits by removing the spring. Now paint both of the wooden parts and leave to dry fully.

2 Once dry, reassemble the peg – if you are confused about what goes where, simply refer to another peg.

3 Fill both sides of your pompom maker with white yarn and make your pompom.

4 Give your pompom a medium to hard trim, retaining the tail ends.

5 Thread one tail end onto the yarn needle. If you have a button with four holes, push the needle from the front to the back through one hole, and back through another hole to the front again. Repeat this with the other tail end in the remaining two holes. If your button has just two holes, feed the two tail ends through so that they end up at the front exiting from opposite holes.

6 Tie the tail ends together firmly with a knot snug between the button and the pompom.

7 Trim the tail ends off flush with the edge of the pompom.

8 Following the manufacturer's instructions, glue the pompom and button to the mouth end of the painted clothes peg.

9 Make a whole collection of pegs to display your cards.

Tip You could clip little handwritten cards in these clothes pegs to use as placements at your dining table.

1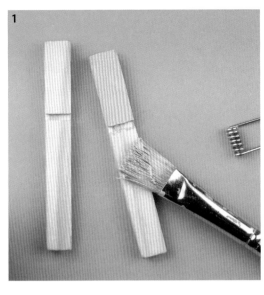

2

3

4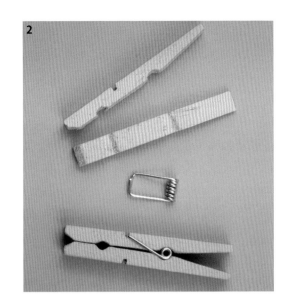

5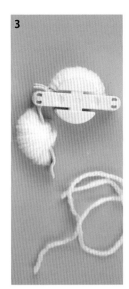

6

7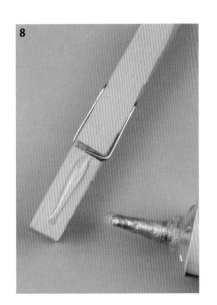

8

9

FLUFFY FAIRY LIGHTS

Customize a set of Christmas lights with these soft, subtly coloured pompoms. They will look great around the frame of a window or door, along the centre of a dining table, or even around the headboard of your bed. You can easily change the character of your lights by varying the size and colour of your pompoms.

YOU WILL NEED
White super chunky yarn
Scraps of white DK yarn for tying
Contrasting colour DK yarns
2½in (6.5cm) pompom maker
Small, sharp scissors
Yarn needle
LED fairy lights

1 Take your pompom maker and wrap it with yarn – use three strands of one of the coloured DK yarns, combined with one strand of the super chunky white yarn to create a speckled pompom, secured with yarn.

2 Give the whole surface of your speckled pompom a soft trim with the sharp scissors. Move aside sections of the white strands of thick yarn in the pompom to isolate strands of coloured yarn, a few strands at a time. Use the very tip of the sharp scissors to trim the coloured yarn by about ⅜–⅝in (1–1.5cm), including the tail ends.

3 Continue working over the whole surface of your pompom until all the colour strands are short and glowing in a 'kernel' of coloured haze within the white, fluffy pompom.

4 Repeat steps 1–3, either using the same colour or as many different colours as you want for your lights.

5 Cut an 8in (20cm) length of white DK yarn and thread it onto your needle. Push the needle through the centre of one of your pompoms, drawing it through to the other side whilst leaving a tail end. Push the needle back through the pompom again, close to the point where it exited.

6 Draw the needle all the way through, remove the needle and pull at the two tail ends to make them of an equal length and lose the loop on the other side of the pompom to disappear into the pile of the coloured yarn. Tie a firm knot with the two tail ends before using them to attach the pompom between two bulbs on your string of LED fairy lights. Do this with a bow if you plan to remove them for storage, or with a knot, trimming the tail ends off, if you want to keep the pompoms on the lights more permanently.

Tip Make sure your fairy lights are the LED kind, which do not get hot when lit. Do not leave the lights on when you are not in the room.

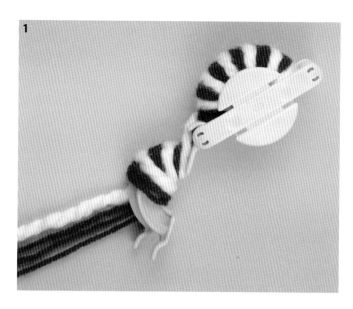

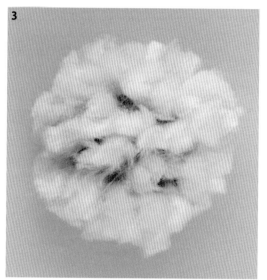

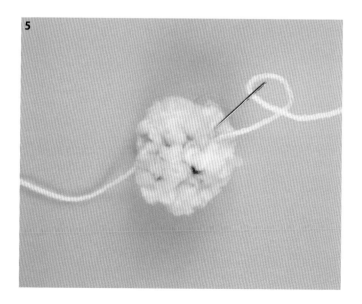

BRIGHT GARLAND

What a great way to announce a celebration! This lovely garland can be made from any number of colours or sizes of pompoms, with a tassel at either end to finish it off. You could try traditional Christmas colours or warm things up with various shades of red, pink and orange.

YOU WILL NEED
For a 5ft (1.5m) long garland:
Red, pink and orange DK yarns
  (or colours of your choice)
Assorted pompom makers: 3⅜in (8.5cm),
  2½in (6.5cm), 1⅝in (4.5cm) and 1⅜in (3.5cm)
5ft (1.5m) of ¹/₁₆in (1.5mm) white cotton
  beading thong
2 x 5in (5 x 12.5cm) scrap card
Small, sharp scissors
Yarn needle

1 Start off by making a number of pompoms. I made: 2 x 3⅜in (8.5cm), 3 x 2½in (6.5cm), 7 x 1⅝in (4.5cm) and 15 x 1⅜in (3.5cm). Give them all a medium trim, cutting off their tail ends.

2 Lay your pompoms out in front of you in a row. Take time to arrange the order you have them in, mixing both colours and sizes in a seemingly random fashion. Thread the cotton thong through the yarn needle and, working from left to right, start threading your pompoms on to the white thong. Hold the pompoms gently but securely in your fist, ensuring you do not pull them apart at all as you draw the needle and thong through them. If you have tied your pompoms tightly when making them, they should retain their position on the thong as you push them along. Move the first pompom down to about 4½in (12cm) from the far end of your thong. Place the subsequent ones slightly apart. If they are a bit close, you may want to tie a knot in the thong either side of each of them. Place the knots snugly below the surface and within the pile of the pompom's wool.

3 When all your balls are threaded, trim your thong to 4½in (12cm) from the last pompom. Set your work aside and make two tassels. Take the piece of card and wrap yarn around its longer length 25 times. Cut the yarn and thread a 12in (30cm) length of it onto your needle. Push the needle under the wraps of yarn.

4 Draw the needle through so that the wraps are lying across the centre of the doubled yarn. Pull the two ends of the yarn to one end of the card and tie them in a tight knot, encircling the fold in the wrapped yarn. Use sharp scissors to cut though the fold at the other ends of the wrapped yarn and remove the card.

5 Take another length of yarn and wrap it four or five times around the cut wraps, about ½in (1.25cm) below the looped and tied top. Trim the ends to the same length with sharp scissors.

6 Thread the two tail ends from step 5 onto your needle and push the needle down through the wraps you made and lose them within the cluster of yarn forming the tassel. Remove the needle and trim the tail ends if they are too long. Now thread the needle back onto the thong and push it through the loop at the top of your tassel and the centre of the wraps below.

7 Draw the needle gently through the wraps and out again among the tails of the tassel. Remove the needle and tie a knot at the end of the thong.

8 Give the thong a gentle tug so that its knot tucks snugly just below the wraps and is nestled within the tassel yarns, where it will be hidden.

9 Thread the two tail ends at the top of the tassel onto the needle and feed it in through the top of your tassel and through the wraps below. Remove the needle.

10 The tassel is now complete. Give the ends another smart trim if they need it.

11 Your garland is now ready to hang along a mantelshelf or around a doorway to add bright, festive cheer to your home.

SNOWFALL SCREEN

A great little project to make with the family! Simply get out all the pompom makers you have and work your way through your white yarn to make a dangling screen for a window or glass door. The different sizes can be put in order – from large at the top to small at the bottom – or simply randomly to create a sweet pastiche of a little snowstorm, which will move delightfully in a breeze.

YOU WILL NEED

For a screen measuring 40 x 41½in (102 x 107cm):

Oddments of white DK yarn

Assorted pompom makers from 3⅜in (8.5cm) to 1in (2.5cm)

Small, sharp scissors

Yarn needle

Small drill bit (to accommodate yarn needle)

Fabric glue

Tape measure

½in (1.25cm) dowelling cut to the required length (see step 1)

White acrylic paint

Paintbrush

Hooks for hanging

Electric hand drill

1 Prepare the hanging rod first. Cut this to the width of your windowpane plus 4in (10cm), or enough to hang it from the window frame on either side. Paint it white.

2 Drill a hole ½in (1.25cm) in from either end of the dowelling for hanging loops. Now mark the position for nine holes along the dowelling for your 'snow falls' to hang from – the two outer holes should be placed 5in (12.5cm) from either end; the remaining seven holes evenly spaced between these two. Using the paint, touch up any areas that may have splintered slightly during the drilling process.

3 Now make all your pompoms. I made: 5 x 3⅜in (8.5cm), 20 x 2½in (6.5cm), 20 x 1⅝in (4.5cm), 20 x 1⅜in (3.5cm) and 7 x 1in (2.5cm). Tie them all off with white yarn and give them a medium trim, cutting off both of the tail ends as you do so.

4 Find a good clear space to work in – you need to lay out all your pompoms and decide the order in which to string them. Divide your pompoms into nine groups with a complete mixture of sizes in each if you are making a random arrangement. Alternatively, you could work from large at the top down to small at the bottom, or large on the outside edges down to small in the middle – or any other arrangement you like, of course. Once you have your groups of 'snow', either take a photo of your arrangement or make a little sketch to refer to while you string them. They need not be evenly spaced as their sizes vary and doing so would possibly look a bit awkward.

5 Now start stringing your pompoms in position, one ball at a time. The drop on my pompoms is 36in (91cm), so I cut yarn this length plus 8in (20cm) to allow for knotting and finishing off. Starting with your first group of pompoms, and with a yarn needle attached to your first length of white yarn, feed the needle through the intended bottom pompom and pull a 5in (12.5cm) tail through to the other side. Re-insert the needle about ¼in (6mm) from where it exited and push it back through to the top of the pompom again. Tie a firm double knot in the yarn at the top of the pompom.

6 Trim the short tail end flush with the pile of the pompom.

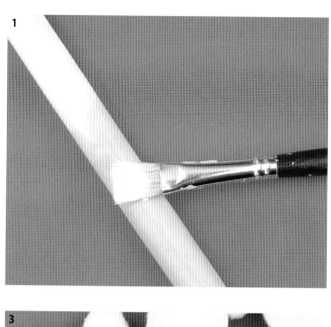

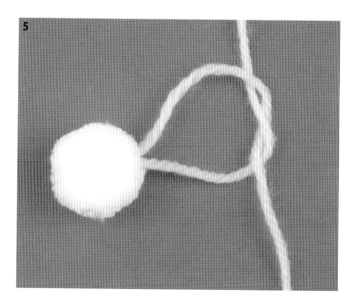

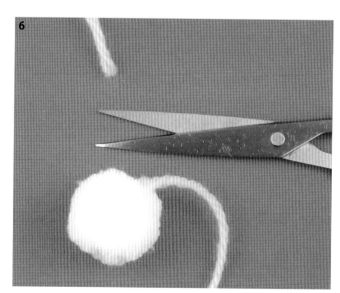

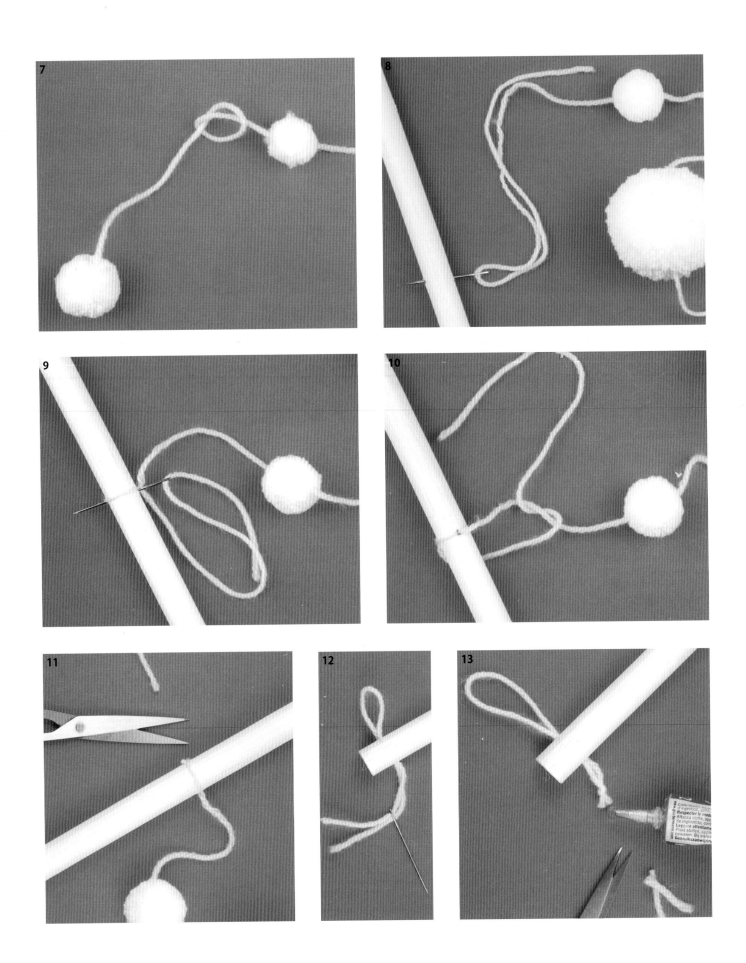

7 Thread the needle back onto the long remaining piece of yarn. Feed the needle through the next pompom – the pompoms should hold the position you push it to, but you can add a knot in the yarn just below it if you like. Continue threading (and knotting) the pompoms until you have completed the first 'fall' of snow.

8 Store your work as you go by hanging over the back of a chair to avoid tangling. Continue repeating steps 5–7 until all your 'falls' are completed. One by one and in the correct order, thread the yarn needle onto the top end of each yarn 'fall' of pompoms and feed them through their corresponding holes in the dowelling. First, you need to push the needle from the bottom to the top.

9 Now draw the yarn though. Use a tape to measure the length from the bottom pompom to the dowelling and pull it through to your required measurement for your finished 'falls'. Bring the needle over the front of the dowelling and up through the hole again from bottom to top.

10 Wrap the yarn around the other side to the bottom again and tie a small and very firm knot just below the dowelling.

11 Push the needle up through the hole from the bottom to the top again. Give the needle a firm tug, so that the knot slips into the bottom of the drilled hole. Cut off the tail end flush with the top surface of the dowelling.

12 Take an 8in (20cm) length of yarn and fold it in half. Thread the two raw ends through a yarn needle and push it through one of the holes drilled at either end for hanging. Leave the loop end protruding at the other side.

13 Remove the needle. Tie a knot in the yarn tails, ½in (1.25cm) from the ends. Trim close to the knot. Put some fabric glue on the knot before tugging the loop gently so that the knot is pulled up into the hole slightly. Leave for the glue to dry and repeat at the other end. Fix a hook at either side of your window and hang your screen.

Tip To keep your Snowfall Screen tidy when you pack it away on Twelfth Night, turn the dowelling so that the falls of pompoms become wound around it.

MATERIALS
& TECHNIQUES

MATERIALS

Each project specifies the supplies you will need for making pompoms, but generally you should simply be able to lay your hands upon the most important items – pompom makers, yarn and very sharp, small scissors.

Yarn

Generally I have used DK yarn in projects – a looser twist in your yarn or a chunkier one will produce a softer and larger ball. Ideally, use wool or acrylic yarns – natural cottons, linens and silks don't have much bounce and spring to them, which makes tying them tightly more of a challenge. Also, the tying strings tend to show and are less likely to become buried in their pile.

Pompom makers

Gone are the days of the cardboard discs, including the frustrating moment when it becomes a struggle to push the yarn through the card's centre. These days you can buy ingeniously designed pompom makers that speed up the making process amazingly. This may be a less romantic and nostalgic way of making pompoms, but I must admit they are incredibly clever little gadgets. They make pompom making a very swift process and are a reliable asset when you are churning out multiple pompoms for a single project. If you are making a large project, they are brilliant. The instructions in this book assume the use of pompom makers, but you can use other methods in their place, as I will also describe here.

TECHNIQUES

MAKING YOUR POMPOMS

Using a pompom maker

Pompom makers come in many sizes – I have used a range of them in these projects from a larger sized 3⅜in (8.5cm) pompom maker, down to a tiny ¾in (2cm) sized one. They all come with instructions, but I'd highly recommend that you have a few trial runs with spare yarn just to get the hang of how they work. The finished sizes will obviously be dictated by the amount of trimming you subject each pompom to! Follow the manufacturer's instructions on the packaging and take a bit of time to fiddle with your pompom maker and get the feel of it.

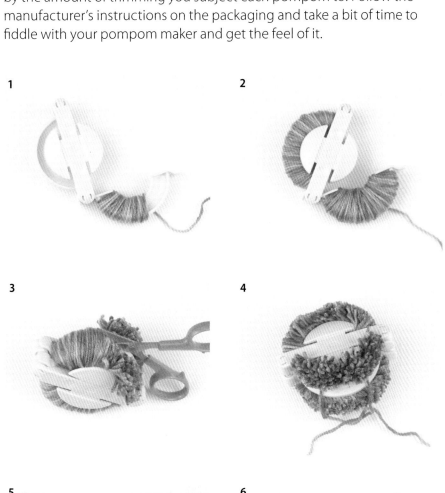

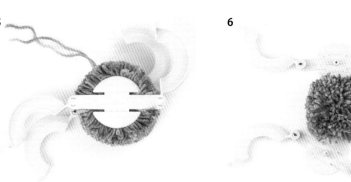

1 Fold out one pair of arches and work methodically, wrapping your yarn around this side evenly.

2 Fold the full arches in, and the remaining empty pair out. Continue the yarn wrapping until this side too is full.

3 Fold this pair of arches back in and cut your yarn. Slip the sharp tip of your scissor's blade in between the two halves of the maker and start snipping around the circumference, taking care to cut through all the wraps of yarn as you do so.

4 Once you have completed cutting all the way around, take a length of yarn and slip it in between the two sides of your pompom maker. Tie a very firm knot, gathering the centre of the yarn wraps tightly as you do so. It's worth wrapping the two yarn tail ends around to the other side and to tie another firm knot there too.

5 Ease each of the four arches out, taking it slowly.

6 Pull the two halves of your maker apart gently to release your pompom. Fluff it up and trim any stray yarns to make it nice and symmetrical.

Traditional pompom making

You don't need to buy a clever little gadget to make your own pompoms. All it takes is card (a cereal packet is perfect), a pair of paper cutting scissors, a ruler, compasses and a pencil, yarn and a yarn needle.

1 Draw a doughnut shape on a scrap of cardboard. The outer circle should measure 1½in (4cm) and the inner circle about ¾in (2cm). Cut it out.

2 Cut out the centre circle then use the doughnut shape as a template to draw another one and cut this out as well.

3 Place your two pieces of card on top of one another and wind your yarn into a smallish ball. Start wrapping the yarn onto the doughnuts, working methodically to cover the card evenly and consistently.

4 Alternatively, you can wrap the yarn on smaller cardboard doughnuts by threading it on a yarn needle and using that.

5 If you run short of yarn while wrapping, simply start a new length of it. If you wind two, three or four threads of yarn at a time, the whole process goes much faster.

6 Continue wrapping round and round until you have used up your yarn. Use a tiny crochet hook to hook the tail end behind a wrap of yarn and hold it in place.

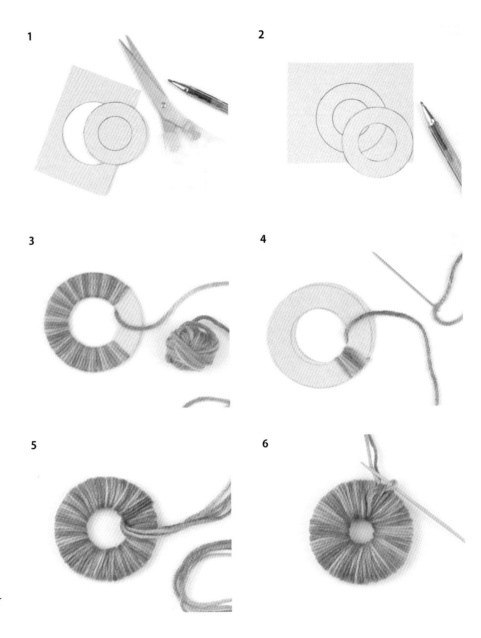

1   2

3   4

5   6

7

8

9

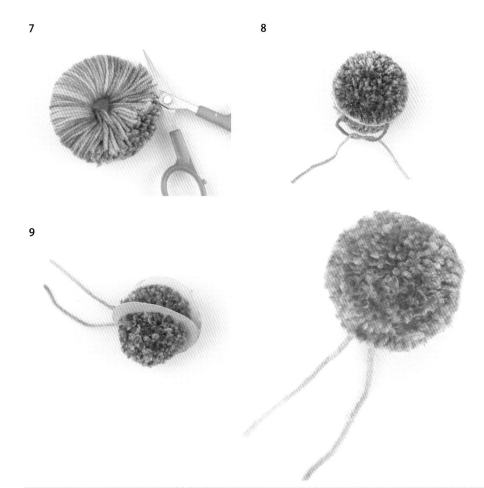

7 Slip the sharp tip of your scissor's blade in between the two card doughnuts and start snipping around the circumference, taking care not to cut the card as you do so.

8 Once you have completed cutting all the way around, take a length of yarn and slip the centre of it in between the two pieces of cardboard. Tie a very firm knot, gathering the centre of the yarn wraps tightly as you do so. It's worth wrapping the two yarn tail ends around to the other side and to tie another firm knot there too.

9 Pull the two pieces of card apart gently (you may even cut them off if you don't intend to use them again) and release your pompom. Fluff up your pompom and trim any stray yarns to make it nice and symmetrical.

Flat plastic pompom makers
These are, in effect, a more durable version of the cardboard doughnuts. They come in pairs and pop apart to give you three different sizes. Use them exactly as you would the old-fashioned cardboard version. Follow the manufacturer's instructions on the packaging.

Making super-quick, multiple pompoms

This is a brilliant way to make multiple pompoms very quickly. I've done these three by winding my yarn around the length of a pad of A4 paper, but you can use the back of a chair, or even two chairs... the longer the length of your initial winding, the more pompoms you can make from it.

1 Wind the yarn around the longer measurement of a pad of A4 paper. Slip the loops of fabric off carefully – you could use a pair of knitting needles, one through each end, to retain the loops and avoid tangles at this point.

2 Take a 6–8in (15–20cm) piece of yarn and tie it around the centre of the wraps and tie a very firm knot.

3 Tie two further lengths of yarn, one in the right of the left-hand edge, and one to the left of the right-hand edge.

4 Use very sharp scissors to cut through the yarn wraps between the middle and right-hand yarn ties.

5 Now cut through the wrapped loops on the right-hand edge. Cut between the central and left-hand ties, and then through the end loops on the left.

6 Finally, give each of your pompoms a trim.

1

2

3

4

5

6

Extra large quick pompoms

1 For an instant make, tie the centre of a whole ball of yarn with several wraps of a length of similar yarn and as firmly as you can.

2 Now snip through the loops at each end to produce a particularly shaggy creation!

3 Get busy with the sharp scissors and even it out a bit – this is more reminiscent of a cheerleader's accessory, but joyfully large and immediate.

Extra small quick pompoms

1 Take a length of yarn and slip it between the prongs of a standard fork. Centre it so that you have an equal length on either side of the fork.

2 Now wrap yarn around the prongs about 15–20 times. Cut the yarn off. Take the two tail ends of your length of yarn and tie firmly around the wraps.

3 Push off the fork and snip the loops at either side to reveal your shaggy little pompom, then trim.

Mixing colours

1 The look of your pompom can be varied by your choice of colour. Wrapping several different colours at a time produces a speckled pompom.

2 Wrapping the two sides of your maker or doughnut in different colours creates a ball with contrasting hemispheres. Or if you follow a chart you can create features and patterns when you wrap your yarn over the pompom maker's arches (see Frosty Snowman, page 24).

1

2

3

1

2

3

1a

1b

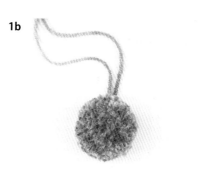

2

Trimming your pompom

Once your pompom is removed from the maker, you need to make the decision of how much to trim it. As you trim, pull the tail ends of your ties away from the blades of your scissors to avoid cutting them off by mistake – if this does happen, do not panic. You can take a length of yarn and a sharp needle, push the needle through the centre of your pompom from front to back, then back through from the back to the front again. Remove the needle before tying it tight with the two yarn tails and burying it deep within the pile of your pompom.

Soft trimming: in the first instance, the pompom will be fairly irregular and shaggy – just the smallest amount of trimming with sharp scissors will give it more symmetry while maintaining the relaxed character.

Medium trimming: taking more off your pompom, turning it as you work and constantly holding it up to check its contours, will give you a neater result, but still maintain a softness to the pompom's silhouette.

Hard trimming: cutting the wool of your pompom back harshly to almost half its initial size will give you a firm, velvety surface, a less 'home-made' and more 'professional' finish.

'Sculpting' your pompoms

Trimming and sculpting pompoms can be simply done boldly and with confidence. If you need a bit more reassurance, there are templates for you to hold your work against during this process. These can, of course, be re-sized to suit your purposes.

Some of the projects here involve 'sculpting' your pompom to create shape and character. It's worth having a practice on a few pompoms first and make sure you use really sharp scissors. It also helps to have an outline template to hold your work up against as you trim – this will let you see where you need to trim further and where you have already done plenty.

Finishing touches

The addition of extras at the completion of a project can add a little special quality to the whole thing, whether felt leaves on holly berries, or a soft feather on a bird, add your own embellishments from any little treasures in your stash. Ribbons, little buttons and bells are especially cute and festive.

TINY FIR TREE,
page 36

OTHER USEFUL TECHNIQUES

Twisted cords

You can use twisted cords to make beaks and noses for birds and snowmen.

1

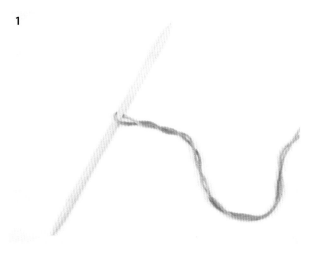

1 Take a 20in (50cm) length of yarn and loop it over a knitting needle, aligning its two ends so that the needle is positioned in the middle of it. Hold the needle still with one hand and start twisting the two yarn ends by rolling them between the finger and thumb of your other hand.

2 You now have a twisted loop of two threads of yarn. Holding the twisting in place, fold this back on itself about 2in (5cm) from the loop on the knitting needle, so that the tail end of the yarn passes over and beyond the now tightened loop. The twisted yarns will naturally wrap fairly snugly into each other, forming a soft, twisted cord.

2

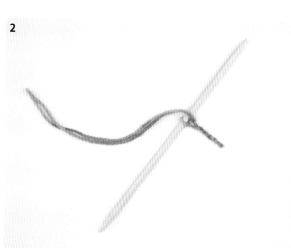

3 Slip the cord off the knitting needle and unravel it to achieve the length you want for your beak or nose – about ½in (1.25cm) – remembering that some of its length will be lost in the pile of the pompom. Thread the tail ends onto a yarn needle to start attaching it to your work.

3

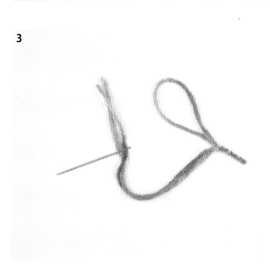

CHEERY SNOWMAN, page 24

Acknowledgements

A big thank you to Neal Grundy for the photography and to Wendy McAngus and everyone else at GMC for their input. Thanks to Erika Knight for her delicious yarns , great friendship and support. Also thanks to a rather feral cat called Missy for keeping me entertained, stealing pompoms from my studio and batting them about my home – she was truly in heaven! Of course, thanks to my friends and family – especially the dear old Dad who joined in making snowball pompoms, rather aptly in a chalet in Kitzbühel, Austria. He hadn't made one since the age of four in Shanghai, when he wasn't allowed to cut it because he was too young – alas, he is now too old!

Resources

Pompom makers

Hobbycraft: www.hobbycraft.co.uk

Yarns

Erika Knight yarns: www.erikaknight.co.uk

Rowan yarns: www.knitrowan.com

Sirdar yarns: www.sirdar.co.uk

Bells

Amazon: www.amazon.co.uk

Hobbycraft: www.hobbycraft.co.uk

Felt and haberdashery

www.thebrightonsewingcentre.co.uk

Beads and cotton thong

www.beadsdirect.co.uk

INDEX

To order a book, or to
request a catalogue, contact:

GMC Publications Ltd,
Castle Place, 166 High Street,
Lewes, East Sussex, BN7 1XU,
United Kingdom

Tel: +44 (0)1273 488005
www.gmcbooks.com